OUR
GRE★T
STATES

WHAT'S GREAT ABOUT
VIRGINIA?

✳ Jamie Kallio

⌞ LERNER PUBLICATIONS COMPANY ✳ MINNEAPOLIS

CONTENTS

Content Consultant: Neil Shumsky, Professor of History, Virginia Tech

Lerner Publications Company
A division of Lerner Publishing Group, Inc.
241 First Avenue North
Minneapolis, MN 55401 USA

For reading levels and more information, look up this title at www.lernerbooks.com.

Main body text set in ITC Franklin Gothic Std Book Condensed 12/15.
Typeface provided by Adobe Systems.

Library of Congress Cataloging-in-Publication Data

Kallio, Jamie.
    What's great about Virginia? / by Jamie Kallio.
        pages   cm. — (Our great states)
    Includes index.
    ISBN 978-1-4677-3341-0 (lib. bdg. : alk. paper)
    ISBN 978-1-4677-4720-2 (eBook)
    1. Virginia—Juvenile literature.
2. Virginia—Guidebooks—Juvenile literature.
I. Title. II. Title: What's great about Virginia?
F226.3.K35 2015
975.5—dc23   2013045904

Manufactured in the United States of America
1 – PC – 7/15/14

VIRGINIA Welcomes You!

Virginia is rich with US history. It was the first colony in what is now the United States. Plan a trip to drop by the Jamestown Settlement or Colonial Williamsburg. Both are living museums. They show what colonial life was like. Or maybe you want to see George Washington's home. Do you like to spend time outside? Virginia has lots of outdoor activities. You will find mountains, beaches, and caves in this exciting state. Go hiking through the mountains. Try camping in the forests. You could explore old caverns. Or you could go sailing on the sea. Read on to learn about ten amazing places you can visit in Virginia. With so much to see and do, you will be glad you came.

OHIO

MARYLAND

WEST VIRGINIA

KENTUCKY

APPALACHIAN PLATEAU

Mount Rogers
(5,729 feet/1,746 m)

Miles
0   20   40
0   20 40 60
Kilometers

North Fork
South Fork
Shenandoah River

DISTRICT OF COLUMBIA

Arlington
Alexandria

Rappahannock River

Potomac River

DELAWARE

Chesapeake Bay

ATLANTIC OCEAN

Natural Bridge

James River

Richmond

BLUE RIDGE MOUNTAINS

N

Roanoke

Williamsburg
Newport News
Portsmouth
Chesapeake

Hampton
Norfolk
Virginia Beach

Roanoke River

TENNESSEE

NORTH CAROLINA

Explore Virginia's beaches and all the places in between! Just turn the page to find out all about the OLD DOMINION. >

5

VIRGINIA AQUARIUM AND MARINE SCIENCE CENTER

> The Virginia Aquarium and Marine Science Center is one of the best aquariums in the country. You'll find it in Virginia Beach. The aquarium has more than three hundred exhibits. The tanks hold 800,000 gallons (3 million liters) of seawater and freshwater. The types of animals will astound you. Harbor seals greet you at the door. Inside, you will see loggerhead turtles and stingrays. Many people like the Ray Touch Pool. You can pet the stingrays when they come to the surface.

If you need a rest, head to the 3-D IMAX Theater. You can watch fun movies about ocean life.

Stop at Virginia Beach's popular boardwalk. It runs along the beaches. No cars drive on this special sidewalk. It is meant for walkers, bikers, and in-line skaters. The boardwalk is lined with stores and restaurants. It also has an amusement park. A fishing dock is nearby. If you get warm, you can swim in the ocean.

Loggerhead turtles are just one of many animals you'll see at the aquarium.

VIRGINIA BEACH

Explorers from England landed in Virginia Beach in 1607. The landing spot is called the First Landing Cross. These men moved on to settle Jamestown. Many early settlers traveling to North America traveled through Virginia Beach. Modern-day Virginia Beach is the largest city in Virginia. It is the 39th largest city by population in the United States.

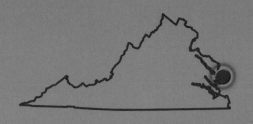

CHINCOTEAGUE PONY SWIM

> Assateague Island in coastal Virginia is a great place to see wild ponies. They have been on the island for hundreds of years. Legend says horses swam to the island long ago. They were cargo on a Spanish ship that sank along the island's coast.

Each July, volunteer firefighters round up the ponies. Then the ponies swim to nearby Chincoteague Island. Many of the ponies are sold at auction. This keeps the island from having too many ponies. About fifty thousand people come to the pony swim and auction each year.

In 1947, Marguerite Henry wrote the children's novel *Misty of Chincoteague*. It is about the Chincoteague Pony Swim. The swim is still a popular event.

While you are on the coast, there are many other great things to do. You can swim or dig for clams. You can even hunt for crabs.

Crabbing is a popular activity in coastal Virginia.

Spectators watch as the ponies swim to Chincoteague Island.

JAMESTOWN SETTLEMENT

> The Jamestown Settlement is a living-history museum. People here dress and act as they did in the 1600s. Jamestown was the first colony founded in North America by the English. It was built in 1607. The colony's name comes from England's King James I.

Jamestown has many places to see. There are also lots of activities to enjoy. Begin at the Powhatan Village. It shows how American Indians lived in the area. You can grind corn. This is how American Indians made cornmeal. You can also wander through the *yehakins*. American Indians made these homes from bent trees. Then they put reed mats on top.

Next, walk the river pier to see replicas of colonial ships. You can climb aboard the *Discovery*, the *Godspeed*, and the *Susan Constant*. Have fun exploring all levels of the ships. How many cannons can you spot on board?

Make sure to stop at James Fort. This is a fenced area shaped like a triangle. It has replicas of the first settlers' homes, a church, and a storehouse. If you have enough time, you can try on armor. You also can watch gun drills.

POCAHONTAS

Chief Powhatan was the ruler of the Powhatan people in Virginia in 1607. His daughter's name was Pocahontas. Pocahontas went to Jamestown often. One of the settlers there was Captain John Smith. He was captured by the Powhatans. It is said Chief Powhatan was going to have Smith killed. Pocahontas threw herself onto Captain Smith. She saved his life. Later, Pocahontas married a settler named John Rolfe. They moved to England.

You'll see traditional Powhatan homes at the Powhatan Village.

VIRGINIA AIR AND SPACE CENTER

> Hampton is the birthplace of the US space program. Don't miss a visit to the Virginia Air and Space Center. There, you will feel the excitement of air and space travel. The center has more than one hundred hands-on exhibits.

In the flight hall, you can jump into the B-24 motion simulator. This allows you to feel like you are flying a World War II bomber plane.

Next, make your way to the space hall. There, you can see giant models of the solar system. You can even view a three-billion-year-old rock from the moon. Or you can feel what it's like to land on the moon in the Lunar Landing Simulator. The space hall also has a time machine. You can watch videos from history. They show exploration from the past, present, and future. At the end of the day, visit the five-story IMAX Theater for more fun.

In the Virginia Air and Space Center you'll see different equipment from years of space travel.

The Apollo 12 landing capsule landed on the moon in 1969.

BUSCH GARDENS
WILLIAMSBURG

> You will not want to miss Virginia's biggest amusement park. With more than fifty rides, this park will make your heart race with excitement all day. Make sure to check out the Apollo's Chariot, Loch Ness Monster, and Alpengeist roller coasters. The Alpengeist sends riders down a 195-foot (59-meter) drop at 67 miles (108 kilometers) per hour!

Visit one of six nation-themed areas for lunch or dinner. You can choose from England, Scotland, Ireland, France, Italy, or Germany. Then visit some of the park's animal displays. Learn more about the gray wolf at Wolf Valley. You can hold a snake or pet an alligator at Jack Hanna's Wild Reserve.

On hot days, visit nearby Water Country USA. There are more than thirty rides and slides where you can cool off. Cruise down the Hubba Hubba Highway on a raft. Try a surfboard in the wave pool. Watch divers in the water acrobatics show. If you feel brave, try one of Vanish Point's four waterslides.

There are many waterslides to choose from at Water Country USA.

The Alpengeist is one of the tallest roller coasters at Busch Gardens.

VIRGINIA MUSEUM OF TRANSPORTATION

The Jupiter rocket, on display at the Virginia Museum of Transportation, is seen here ready for launch in 1959.

> If you like to travel, the Virginia Museum of Transportation is for you. This museum has more than fifty trains in the rail yard. See steam engines and diesel trains. The museum even has a bright red train caboose. This collection of trains is the largest in the South.

In the road gallery, you will find old-time cars, trucks, and an ambulance. You can see the Jupiter Rocket in the Air and Space gallery. The United States first launched this rocket into space in 1956. The gallery also has many types of planes. You can even look inside a private jet.

When you have seen all the galleries, be sure to view the model trains. The first is an O-gauge model train layout with four levels, six tracks, and many train cars. It has more than 600 feet (183 m) of track. You also will want to visit the model circus train. Real circus trains used special railcars to move animals from place to place. You can see how elephants traveled by train.

This rare diesel train was recently restored by the museum.

COLONIAL WILLIAMSBURG

> Colonial Williamsburg is one of the largest living-history museums in the world. Williamsburg was the largest and wealthiest city in Virginia during the 1700s. It was also the most populated city. Here you can take a look back in time at how people lived long ago. Workers dress in 1700s clothing and show tourists around. Workers explain what life was like in the 1770s before the American Revolution (1775–1783).

Wander the streets to see the courthouse and the wigmaker. You can visit the apothecary (pharmacy) and the shoemaker too. There are games you can play. Or you can take lessons from a colonial dancing master. Take part in a military drill or help fire a cannon. Take a carriage ride through town. There is also a candlelight tour through homes and shops.

Carriages bring people around town (*above*). Make sure to stop at the shoe shop (*below*).

NATURAL BRIDGE

> The Natural Bridge is found in Rockbridge County. The bridge is a limestone formation caused by erosion from Cedar Creek. The bridge has a natural arch that is 215 feet (66 m) high and 90 feet (27 m) wide. It was a sacred place to the Monacan American Indians. At one time, Thomas Jefferson owned the bridge. In 1750, George Washington cut his initials in the bridge.

After you see the Natural Bridge, there are many other fun activities nearby for you to try. Tour a historical American Indian village. The village shows visitors what life was like for American Indians three hundred years ago. You will learn how American Indians fished, cooked, built homes, and more.

You can hike along Cedar Creek Nature Trail. Keep your camera handy. You'll want to take pictures of Lace Falls. Keep an eye out for the fifteen-hundred-year-old tree along the trail. Do not be surprised if a wild turkey or deer run past.

AMERICAN INDIANS

Virginia recognizes eight American Indian nations in the state. They are the Pamunkey, Mattaponi, Upper Mattaponi, Chickahominy, Eastern Chickahominy, Monacan, Nansemond, and the Rappahannock nations. Many American Indians still have powwows. A powwow is an American Indian ceremony or social gathering. There is food, dancing, and singing. The Monacans, one of Virginia's oldest nations, hold a powwow in late May.

The Natural Bridge has long been known for the caverns nearby, as shown in this historical photo.

MOUNT VERNON

> Get ready to visit the first president's home and gardens. Make sure to tour all twenty-three galleries and theaters. You can see three wax figures of President George Washington. Each shows him at a different time in his life. Then be sure to watch an action-adventure film about the American Revolution in the museum's theater. Unexpected things happen in this theater. You will feel your chair rumble. You will also watch snow drift down.

In the Hands-On History Center, you can wear colonial costumes. You can also try colonial activities. Play with a dollhouse. Or sit and relax as a storyteller shares stories about Washington and his family.

Be sure to wear your walking shoes to Mount Vernon. You will be going on an adventure. Pick up an Adventure Map with a puzzle in it. You will need to visit nine areas on the grounds to solve the puzzle. When you finish, stop at the gift shop for a prize.

No visit to Mount Vernon would be complete without a stop at the Pioneer Farm. You can grind corn and hoe a field. You also can visit horses, mules, and oxen in the big barn.

Try on colonial clothes before exploring the rest of Mount Vernon.

EIGHT PRESIDENTS

One of Virginia's nicknames is Mother of Presidents. It was home to eight men who became president of the United States. Those men were George Washington, Thomas Jefferson, James Madison, James Monroe, William Henry Harrison, John Tyler, Zachary Taylor, and Woodrow Wilson.

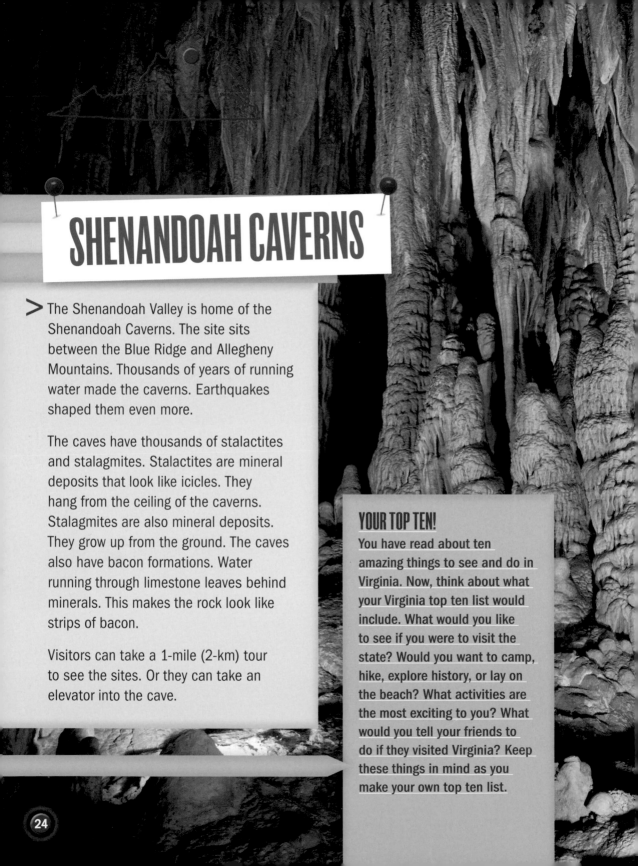

SHENANDOAH CAVERNS

> The Shenandoah Valley is home of the Shenandoah Caverns. The site sits between the Blue Ridge and Allegheny Mountains. Thousands of years of running water made the caverns. Earthquakes shaped them even more.

The caves have thousands of stalactites and stalagmites. Stalactites are mineral deposits that look like icicles. They hang from the ceiling of the caverns. Stalagmites are also mineral deposits. They grow up from the ground. The caves also have bacon formations. Water running through limestone leaves behind minerals. This makes the rock look like strips of bacon.

Visitors can take a 1-mile (2-km) tour to see the sites. Or they can take an elevator into the cave.

YOUR TOP TEN!

You have read about ten amazing things to see and do in Virginia. Now, think about what your Virginia top ten list would include. What would you like to see if you were to visit the state? Would you want to camp, hike, explore history, or lay on the beach? What activities are the most exciting to you? What would you tell your friends to do if they visited Virginia? Keep these things in mind as you make your own top ten list.

You'll see many stalactites and stalagmites as you walk through the caverns.

The Shenandoah Valley is full of beautiful scenery.

25

VIRGINIA BY MAP

> MAP KEY

- ⬡ Capital city
- ○ City
- ◎ Point of interest
- ▲ Highest elevation
- –·– State border

Visit www.lerneresource.com to learn more about the state flag of Virginia.

OHIO

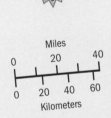

Miles
0   20   40
0   20   40   60
Kilometers

KENTUCKY

APPALACHIAN PLATEAU

Mount Rogers
(5,729 feet/1,746 m)
▲

TENNESSEE

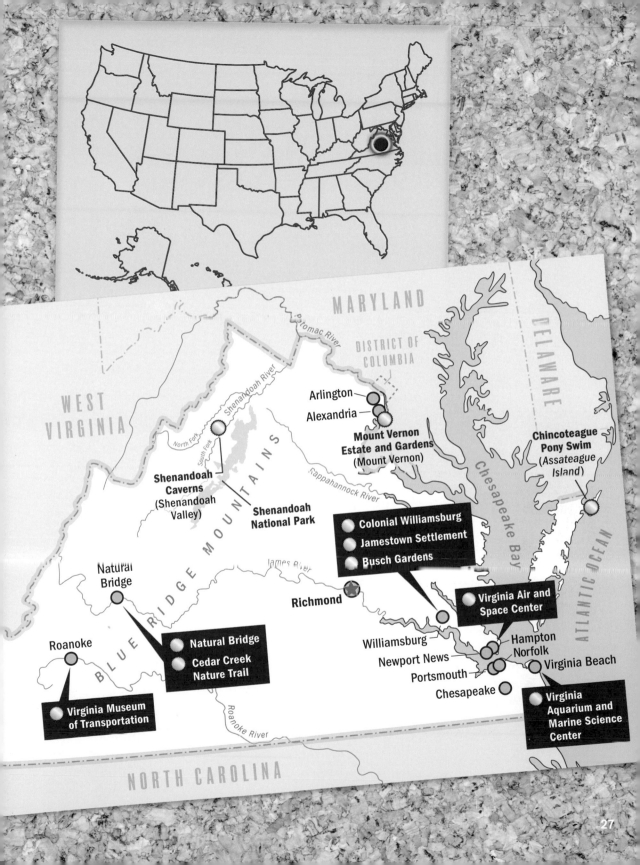

MARYLAND

DISTRICT OF
COLUMBIA

DELAWARE

WEST
VIRGINIA

Potomac River

Shenandoah River

North Fork

South Fork

Shenandoah
Caverns
(Shenandoah
Valley)

Shenandoah
National Park

Rappahannock River

Arlington

Alexandria

Mount Vernon
Estate and Gardens
(Mount Vernon)

Chincoteague
Pony Swim
(Assateague
Island)

Chesapeake Bay

B L U E   R I D G E   M O U N T A I N S

James River

Colonial Williamsburg

Jamestown Settlement

Busch Gardens

Natural
Bridge

Richmond

Virginia Air and
Space Center

ATLANTIC OCEAN

Roanoke

Natural Bridge

Cedar Creek
Nature Trail

Williamsburg

Newport News

Portsmouth

Hampton

Norfolk

Virginia Beach

Chesapeake

Virginia Museum
of Transportation

Roanoke River

Virginia
Aquarium and
Marine Science
Center

NORTH CAROLINA

VIRGINIA FACTS

NICKNAMES: Old Dominion or Mother of Presidents

SONG: "Carry Me Back to Old Virginia" by James A. Bland (song retired in 1997)

MOTTO: *Sic Semper Tyrannis*, or "Thus Always to Tyrants"

FLOWER: dogwood

> **TREE:** flowering dogwood

BIRD: northern cardinal

ANIMAL: American foxhound

> **FOOD(S):** ham, seafood, peanuts

DATE/RANK OF STATEHOOD: June 25, 1788; the 10th state

> **CAPITAL:** Richmond

AREA: 42,774 square miles (110,784 sq. km)

AVERAGE JANUARY TEMPERATURE: 42°F (6°C)

AVERAGE JULY TEMPERATURE: 78°F (26°C)

POPULATION AND RANK: 8,185,867; 12th (2012)

MAJOR CITIES AND POPULATIONS: Virginia Beach (447,021), Norfolk (245,782), Chesapeake (228,417), Arlington (212,900), Richmond (210,309)

NUMBER OF US CONGRESS MEMBERS: 11 representatives, 2 senators

NUMBER OF ELECTORAL VOTES: 13

NATURAL RESOURCES: coal, forests, fisheries

> **AGRICULTURAL PRODUCTS:** beef cattle, corn, eggs, milk, soybeans, turkeys, wheat

MANUFACTURED GOODS: transportation equipment, pharmaceutical products, synthetic fabrics, plastics, rubber products

STATE HOLIDAYS/CELEBRATIONS: George Washington Birthday Celebration, Shenandoah Apple Blossom Festival, Mattaponi Indian Reservation Powwow, State Fair of Virginia

GLOSSARY

apothecary: a druggist, or a pharmacy

auction: a public sale at which things are sold to those who offer to pay the most

cornmeal: a food ground from corn

erosion: the action or process of being worn away by natural forces

marine: relating to the sea

powwow: an American Indian ceremony or social gathering

reed: a tall, thin grass that grows in wet areas

replica: a copy that is exact in all details

simulator: a machine used to show what something looks or feels like. A simulator is usually used for study or to train people.

transportation: a way of traveling from one place to another place

LERNER
e
SOURCE™

Expand learning beyond the printed book. Download free, complementary educational resources for this book from our website, www.lerneresource.com.

FURTHER INFORMATION

Colonial Williamsburg
http://www.history.org/kids/index.cfm
Everything you ever wanted to know and more about Colonial Williamsburg is on this website, including a special kids' section.

Jensen, Niels R. *Virginia*. Edina, MN: Abdo Publishing, 2010. Find out even more about Virginia with this book that touches on popular sports and entertainment.

King, David C., and Stephanie Fitzgerald. *Virginia.* New York: Marshall Cavendish Benchmark, 2011. This book gives an in-depth look at the history of Virginia, as well as some of its historic landmarks.

Official Tourism Website of the Commonwealth of Virginia
http://www.virginia.org/coolplacesforkids
This website is chock-full of tourist information and will help you plan your trip. There is even a section that lists cool places for kids to visit.

The Official Website of the Commonwealth of Virginia
http://www.virginia.gov
The official website of the state includes everything you would ever want to know about Virginia and more.

Ransom, Candice. *Why Did English Settlers Come to Virginia? And Other Questions about the Jamestown Settlement.* Minneapolis: Lerner Publications, 2011. Learn more about the early colonists, why they left England, and how they survived in a new land.

INDEX

PHOTO ACKNOWLEDGMENTS

The images in this book are used with the permission of: © sborisov/iStockphoto, p. 1; © chrisjo/iStockphoto, p. 4; © alphtran/iStockphoto, pp. 4–5; © Laura Westlund/Independent Picture Service, pp. 5, 26–27, 26 (bottom); © Vicki Cronis/Virginian-Pilot/AP Images, pp. 6–7; © Filip Fuxa/Shutterstock Images, p. 7 (left); © spirit of america/Shutterstock Images, p. 7 (right); © Ken Schulze/Shutterstock Images, pp. 8–9; © Scott Neville/AP Images, p. 9 (left); © Apaterson/Shutterstock Images, p. 9 (right); © Visions of America/Glow Images, pp. 10–11; © George Alfred Williams, p. 10; © iStockphoto/Thinkstock, pp. 11, 14–15, 15 (bottom), 18–19; © Mark & Audrey Gibson/Glow Images, pp. 12–13; © Buddy Mays/Corbis/Glow Images, p. 13 (left); © Mark E. Gibson/Corbis/Glow Images, p. 13 (right); © Scott K. Brown/Water Country USA/AP Images, p. 15 (top); © Stephanie Klein-Davis/The Roanoke Times/AP Images, pp. 16–17; NASA, p. 16; © Virginia Museum of Transportation/AP Images, p. 17; © vgoodrich/iStockphoto, pp. 19 (top), 19 (bottom); © dmvphotos/Shutterstock Images, pp. 20–21; © Catherine Lane/iStockphoto, p. 20; Library of Congress, pp. 21 (LC-D4-500570), 23 (bottom) (LC-D416-441); © PhotosbyAndy/Shutterstock Images, pp. 22–23; © Jacquelyn Martin/AP Images, p. 23 (top); © George Allen Penton/Shutterstock Images, pp. 24–25; © Ken Rygh Creative Art & Design/iStockphoto, p. 25 (top); © Cameron Whitman/iStockphoto, p. 25 (bottom); © duncan1890/iStockphoto, p. 26; © Toni Scott/iStockphoto, p. 29 (top); © vladm/iStockphoto, p. 29 (middle, top); © nashvilledino2/iStockphoto, p. 29 (middle, bottom); © pkripper503/iStockphoto, p. 29 (bottom).

Cover: © iStockphoto.com/JuniperCreek (ponies); © Marlene Frazier/Dreamstime.com (Natural Bridge); © Carolyn M Carpenter/Shutterstock.com (Mt. Vernon); © Digital Vision/Photodisc/Thinkstock (Pentagon); © Laura Westlund/Independent Picture Service (map); © iStockphoto.com/fpm (seal); © iStockphoto.com/vicm (pushpins); © iStockphoto.com/benz190 (cork board).